WOBURN HiLL

WEYBRIDG

*A spell for
Miss Grimscuttle*

A spell for
Miss Grimscuttle
by Jo Furminger

Illustrated by Sally Holmes

HODDER AND STOUGHTON
LONDON SYDNEY AUCKLAND TORONTO

To Florence and Betty, who cheerfully
survived my early teaching.

British Library Cataloguing in Publication Data

Furminger, Jo
  A spell for Miss Grimscuttle.
  I. Title
  823'.9'1J   PZ7.F/

  ISBN 0-340-23208-0

First published 1979
Third impression 1984

Published by Hodder and Stoughton Children's Books,
a division of Hodder and Stoughton Ltd, Mill Road,
Dunton Green, Sevenoaks, Kent TN13 2YJ

Printed in Great Britain by St Edmundsbury Press,
Bury St Edmunds, Suffolk

Contents

Chapter One

THE SPELL

One day, although Miss Grimscuttle didn't know it, a spell was cast upon her on her way to school. It happened like this. She was a bit late setting out from home, so that by the time she boarded the morning train it was already fairly full, and since she hated crowds, Miss Grimscuttle stalked along the corridor until she found a compartment occupied only by one homely-looking woman.

'How do you do?' nodded the woman, politely. Miss Grimscuttle sat opposite her with a rather hostile sniff and stared pointedly out of the window, as she never encouraged conversation with strangers.

'Hoity-toity!' thought the woman, whose name was Mrs Boffy, and turning away she began to contemplate pleasanter things, putting the disagreeable schoolteacher out of her mind.

6

Now, Miss Grimscuttle couldn't be blamed
for not knowing, because hardly anybody did,
that Mrs Boffy was a witch, and that morning
she was actually on her way to attend the World
Convention of Witches that was being held on
Hallowe'en. Mrs Boffy had earlier considered

travelling at night by broomstick, which was her favourite means of transport, but in late October the nights can be rather damp and chilly, and at the age of three hundred and seventy-nine she had a tendency to rheumatism during the autumn and winter months.

So Mrs Boffy had finally decided to go by train instead, and since witches almost never go anywhere without their familiars, Mrs Boffy was accompanied by hers, a very sleek and handsome jet black cat called Peterkin.

Until Miss Grimscuttle's arrival, Peterkin had been curled up fast asleep and totally invisible in a corner. But being, like the rest of his tribe, an exceedingly inquisitive animal, hardly had Miss Grimscuttle settled down before he materialised on the seat beside her and stared into her face in a friendly way.

'Aaaagh!' screeched Miss Grimscuttle, who hated cats. She shuddered. 'Where did that animal come from?'

'Oh, you mean Peterkin?' smiled Mrs Boffy pleasantly. 'He's quite harmless, I assure you.'

'Nevertheless, animals are not permitted to travel in public carriages,' retorted Miss Grim-

8

scuttle, eyes a-flash with anger behind her steel spectacles. 'It should be in a proper container in the guard's van at the rear of the train.'

'Oh I couldn't do that to Peterkin,' said Mrs Boffy mildly. 'He wouldn't like it.'

'Whatever do you mean?' cried Miss Grimscuttle. 'It wouldn't do him any harm, and besides, cats are too stupid to understand.'

'Not *my* cat,' insisted Mrs Boffy, but ignoring her Miss Grimscuttle went on, 'If you don't remove it immediately, I shall call the guard.'

Mrs Boffy gave Miss Grimscuttle a pitying smile, and Peterkin sat gazing up at her from inscrutable yellow eyes shot with darting green fires. Miss Grimscuttle was almost choking with anger when suddenly a ticket collector appeared in the doorway. She leapt up.

'You have come just in time, my good man!' she cried. 'Kindly ask this person to remove her cat to the guard's van at ONCE!'

The ticket collector stared round the carriage and then back at Miss Grimscuttle with a perplexed expression on his face.

'What cat, Missus?' he asked.

'That one there!' screamed Miss Grimscuttle,

and turning, she stabbed her finger at the empty space where Peterkin had been sitting only seconds before.

'It must be hiding somewhere!' exclaimed Miss Grimscuttle, peering wildly about her.

'Did you see where it went, Missus?' the ticket collector appealed to Mrs Boffy. But Mrs Boffy, without answering, assumed a foolish smile and pretended that she was deaf.

After a thorough search of the compartment at

Miss Grimscuttle's insistence, and of course finding not so much as a whisker, the ticket collector hastily left, forgetting to clip their tickets in his anxiety to get away. Peterkin wisely remained invisible, and ten minutes later, as the train drew into Blank Street Station, Miss Grimscuttle got up to go.

Now, if she had just left without a word, all would have been well. But she couldn't resist snapping over her shoulder at Mrs Boffy, 'I don't

know where you are hiding that horrid cat, but I hope somebody catches you with it soon.' And with that she flounced through the door.

'You can come out now,' said Mrs Boffy to Peterkin, who appeared on the luggage rack, a bit at a time, finishing with his tail which he proceeded to wash vigorously. Mrs Boffy thought for a minute, then she opened the window and leaned out. She saw Miss Grimscuttle's sparse and bony figure striding away down the platform, and putting her hand out of the window, Mrs Boffy caught up a fistful of autumn wind. Then, whispering some extremely powerful magic words over the trapped air, she blew it after Miss Grimscuttle's retreating back. At a signal from his mistress, Peterkin left the luggage rack and descended lightly on to the dusty platform. Growing gradually more transparent with every step until finally he vanished altogether, he ran silently behind Miss Grimscuttle.

Mrs Boffy carefully closed the window, and smiling with satisfaction she leaned contentedly back in her seat.

'That will teach you to think before you speak,' she said, 'and *never* to be rude to witches.'

12

And Miss Grimscuttle, hurrying quite un-
awares towards Blank Street School, turned up
the collar of her coat against a sudden icy little
breeze which appeared from nowhere to dance
around her ears.

Chapter Two

THE GREEN FINGERS

Later that morning, when the children in her class had finished their mathematics, Miss Grimscuttle indicated a row of brown paper bags on her desk and said, 'I have here a selection of spring flowers. These are daffodil bulbs, these are crocus corms, these are snowdrops and these anemones. I shall choose a small group of *sensible* children to come out and help me plant them on our little plot in the school garden, and the rest of

14

you will get out your English Grammar text books and start at exercise fifteen.'

Miss Grimscuttle's pale eyes roved over the class.

'I'll take Paul, Susan, Andrew, Ben, William and Mary,' she said.

'I shall put my bulbs in a little pattern,' said Susan, as they hurried to the cloakroom to don coats and scarves. 'Like they do in the park in town.'

'I'm going to put mine in rows, in the order that they'll flower,' said William. 'Snowdrops first, crocuses next —'

'Stop that talking and come along,' snapped Miss Grimscuttle, poking her long nose round the door.

15

When the children got outside they discovered to their dismay that they weren't to be allowed to plant the bulbs after all. Their job was merely to dig the ground, which had been hardened by a slight overnight frost, pick out all the biggest stones, and then rake the soil smooth. After that they had to stand by and watch, while Miss Grimscuttle made holes with a little trowel and put in the bulbs where she wanted them to go.

'Please Miss,' said Susan forlornly, 'can't we do just a *few* each?'

'Certainly not!' exclaimed Miss Grimscuttle, coming to the end of a row of daffodils. 'If I do it myself, I'm sure that it will be done properly. Anyway, I know that if *I* plant them, they'll grow, because *I've* got green fingers.'

She had scarcely finished speaking when from somewhere quite near by came a sudden plaintive miaow.

'A cat!' cried Miss Grimscuttle. 'Where is it? The wretched creature will dig holes all over the place. Send it away!'

Everybody looked round, but there was nothing to be seen. Then, a small breeze, heavy with the scent of may, came up from nowhere. It

16

blew gently across the faces of the puzzled children, then just as quickly, died away.

Miss Grimscuttle tutted with annoyance.

'I hope we're not going to have a wretched cat walking all over our garden,' she said. 'Anybody who sees it must chase it away.' She straightened up. The wind had blown a bit of grit into her eye, and she pulled off one of her gardening gloves to wipe it away. The children who noticed first drew in sharp breaths of astonishment. Susan clapped a hand over her mouth.

'Crumbs!' exclaimed William.

'Oh gosh!' said Ben, and couldn't suppress a giggle.

'Whatever is the matter now?' asked Miss Grimscuttle, turning to stare.

'Oh Miss,' said Mary, 'look at your fingers!'

Miss Grimscuttle looked down, then she gaped and gave a little squawk of shock, for every one of her fingers and each of her thumbs was bright green.

'Oh, wherever did that come from?' she muttered in annoyance, picking up her gardening gloves and shaking them as if she expected them to be full of green paint. Of course they weren't, so she took out her handkerchief to scrub at her fingers, and immediately the handkerchief, which was white with blue borders, turned green.

'Dear me!' gasped Miss Grimscuttle, putting a hand to her cheek in bewilderment. 'This is very strange! It appears that some kind of dye has got into my gardening gloves, but I can't think how. I'd better go and wash it off.'

She took her hand down from her face, and the children stared, fascinated, at the big round patch

18

that had appeared on her skin, like green rouge.

'Oh Miss Grimscuttle,' said Susan, 'it's on your cheek now.'

Miss Grimscuttle's eyes bulged and in a croaking voice she said, 'I'm going in right away, but I'll leave you in charge out here till I get back, Susan.'

Briefly she rested a hand on Susan's head and then turned to dash with long, stiff strides across the playground to the teachers' washroom. She was too busy with her own desperate thoughts to notice the thin wail that rose up behind her, as the children who were left standing in the garden informed Susan that her beautiful mop of golden curls had turned a vivid green.

Halfway across the playground Miss Grimscuttle was waylaid by a boy who carried a piece of paper on which was a note for all the teachers to read. It was from Mr Meek the Headmaster, warning them of the impending visit of an Inspector called Mr Clodworthy, and at the bottom of the paper Mr Meek had left a space for all the teachers to sign their names when they had read it. Miss Grimscuttle, full to the very brim with anxiety to be rid of the green from her

19

fingers, seized the note, scanned through it rapidly, muttered with annoyance beneath her breath then signed and thrust the paper and pencil back at the boy. Then without a backward glance she continued her headlong journey, leaving the boy gazing open-mouthed at his once blue, now green pencil, and once white now green paper, and also the grass-green tip of one of his thumbs that Miss Grimscuttle had happened to touch.

Hurtling through the heavy swing doors at the end of the corridor Miss Grimscuttle nearly collided with one of the older girls who was just coming out of a near-by classroom.

'Look where you're going, child!' snarled Miss Grimscuttle, gripping the girl's arm and whirling her out of the way. The girl gave a little gasp and walked on, rubbing hard at the wide band of green that had appeared on her arm after Miss Grimscuttle had released it.

Although the distraught teacher travelled quickly it wasn't quite quickly enough, because before she could reach the washroom the bell sounded for morning break, and from eight classroom doors poured dozens of children of all ages and sizes, anxious to get into the playground.

As the corridor was very narrow, some of them simply couldn't avoid bumping into Miss Grimscuttle, who put out her hands to steer them away, with the result that a whole crowd of children with various spots and blobs of green soon came to the notice of the teacher on duty outside, and she began to realise that something very strange must have happened.

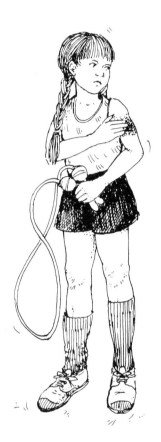

21

Meanwhile Miss Grimscuttle barged into the washroom, turning the brass door-handle green. She rushed to the washbasin and thrust the plug, which immediately became green, into the plug-hole. She turned on the taps which changed to green. Water splashed into the white basin and she plunged in her hands, only to discover that both water and basin took on the same green hue, so did the tablet of pink soap, the brown scrubbing brush, a second lot of water, and finally, the yellow towel on which Miss Grimscuttle frantically dried her hands.

'Oh, oh!' she moaned, and two large tears of anger and frustration slid down her cheeks. She put up a hand to brush them away, and stopped just in time. In her classroom was her handbag, and in the handbag, a pair of gloves. Unable to think further than covering up those dreadful green fingers, Miss Grimscuttle sped down the corridor and almost fell in through the classroom door.

Chapter Three

NURSE TO THE
RESCUE

Mr Meek was just enjoying his cup of morning coffee when there was a loud commotion outside his study. Assuming his sternest expression he yanked open the door and his jaw dropped in amazement as he surveyed the crowd of children congregated there. A young teacher, whose name was Miss Chuckleton, was with them.

'I thought you ought to see these people, Mr Meek,' she said. 'They've all gone green in different places, and it won't come off.'

Altogether there were seventeen victims of Miss Grimscuttle's green fingers, including Susan who was still weeping over the transformation of her lovely golden hair, and one boy who had got a green eye, having been accidentally poked in it during Miss Grimscuttle's frantic rush to the washroom.

Mr Meek took a hasty step backwards, deciding that whatever it was they had, he didn't intend to catch it.

'Er, have you tried disinfectant?' he asked Miss Chuckleton. She nodded.

'And they've all washed and washed,' she said, 'but it won't budge. William says Miss Grimscuttle did it.'

A sly little smile of satisfaction crept over Miss Chuckleton's face as she spoke, because she didn't like Miss Grimscuttle either.

'Does anyone know where Miss Grimscuttle is?' asked Mr Meek.

'Please sir, I saw her in the classroom a minute ago,' volunteered Ben, who had come along with William and Mary just to watch.

'I think we had better go and see what she has to say about this,' said Mr Meek, and keeping at a safe distance, he shepherded the children away.

But Miss Grimscuttle had absolutely nothing to say. She stood defiantly behind her desk staring at Mr Meek with tight lips, her hands encased in leather gloves (fur-lined) which had once been black but were now green, and the cheek that wasn't green was bright red with anger.

They might have remained there all morning wondering what to do if it hadn't been for Miss Chuckleton suddenly remembering that she had seen the School Nurse going in to the Infants.

'Shall I fetch her?' Miss Chuckleton asked. 'She might be able to suggest something.'

Mr Meek, who was standing by an open window hoping that the cold air would kill the green germs, nodded gratefully. Miss Grimscuttle folded herself up in her chair with her back to everybody, and sulked.

Soon the sound of brisk footsteps heralded the return of Miss Chuckleton with the School Nurse, who wore a navy blue hat and coat and carried a large black bag, the sight of which made them all instantly feel better, because it looked as though it were packed full of medicines, ointments and potions to cure every disease that had ever been discovered as well as some that hadn't.

'Right!' said the nurse cheerfully, dumping her bag on the table. 'Let's have a look and see what you've been doing to yourselves.'

28

She examined everybody's green patch in turn, and meanwhile William, Ben and Mary told her what had happened in the garden, and what Miss Grimscuttle had said about having green fingers.

'Ah,' said the nurse, who was very down-to-earth, having five children of her own. She stared penetratingly at Miss Grimscuttle, who was trying to hide her green gloved hands from sight and not succeeding at all. 'Looks to me like a case of Collective Hallucination, brought on by Chronic Auto-Suggestion.'

This sounded so serious that poor Mr Meek, already frozen to the marrow by the window, turned even colder.

'Oh my goodness!' he gasped. 'Can it be cured?'

All the children stared at the nurse in hope and dread, particularly Susan and the boy with the one green eye.

'Of course!' said the nurse, and there was an enormous single sigh of relief from seventeen mouths. Even Miss Grimscuttle's back seemed to become a fraction straighter.

'There's some extremely magic ointment that

29

I keep especially for occasions such as this,' said the nurse, bending over her bag, which, unknown to everyone else, contained not a vast medical kit, but her morning groceries. She rummaged around among onions and potatoes, sauce and sausages, currant cake, cheese and various other items until she found a carton bearing the label, 'Best English Margarine'. Without taking it out of her bag she eased off the lid and scooped up a liberal blob on her finger. Then smoothing the pale yellow grease between the palms of her hands, she rubbed it vigorously into Susan's hair.

Slowly, before their astonished and delighted eyes, Susan's hair resumed its normal golden colour, and when all the green had quite disappeared, she gave one last, huge sniff, and broke into an enormous smile.

The children cheered and jostled forward, while the nurse worked speedily until all the green patches had gone, and so had almost all of her Best English Margarine. But fortunately there was just enough left for Miss Grimscuttle, who came last of all, and very slowly, holding out her green fingers with a look of anguish on her bony face.

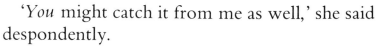

'*You* might catch it from me as well,' she said despondently.

'Rubbish,' replied the nurse, scraping out the remains of the margarine and spreading it deftly over Miss Grimscuttle's hands. 'Nurses never catch anything, it's a well-known fact.'

With a mixture of joy and disbelief, Miss Grimscuttle stared down as her hideous fingers grew paler and paler until all the green was gone. Then briskly disposing of Miss Grimscuttle's green cheek with the final smear of her margarine, the nurse zipped up her bag and saying goodbye to the children, went off to the shops to buy some more.

As everybody rushed outside to enjoy the last five minutes of playtime and Mr Meek retired thankfully to the warmth of his cosy study, Miss Grimscuttle scurried anxiously back to the washroom. She gazed at the doorknob, which winked back at her, brassily, with never a hint of green in sight. Then she forced herself to push open the door and peer inside. Everything was back to normal, soap, washbasin, scrubbing brush, taps and towel. Suddenly feeling a rather severe headache coming on, she hurried back

32

to the classroom and sat down.

'Well, what do you make of all that?' asked Ben, as he and William and Mary congregated beneath their favourite tree on the edge of the playground.

'It was magic,' said William, with conviction.

'Oooh, do you really think so?' asked Mary.

'You mean, someone's cast a spell on her?' said Ben, raising his eyebrows.

'You can bet your Sunday hat on it,' declared William. 'I expect she was rude to somebody in her usual way, and didn't realise the person was a witch, or wizard, or something.'

'In that case,' said Ben with a grin, 'the Green Fingers business probably isn't the end of it, and there's more magic to come.'

And do you know, he was absolutely right.

Chapter Four

THE FLYING LESSON

Miss Grimscuttle's Physical Training Session was the first to be inspected on the day that Mr Clodworthy arrived. Mr Meek, who had cherished a lifelong ambition to be made a School Inspector himself, and who secretly practised fierce expressions in front of his mirror just in case, brought him in to the Hall.

The children were already there, shivering a bit because the Hall was large and rather draughty, and after introducing Mr Clodworthy as quickly as possible Mr Meek hurried back to his office, where he moved his chair closer to the fire. Standing by that wretched window a few days before had given him an awful cold.

'Right, everybody should be standing perfectly still!' cried Miss Grimscuttle, clapping her hands, and nobody did anything, because they already were. From the corner of her eye Miss

34

Grimscuttle glimpsed Mr Clodworthy's little smile of amusement, and frantically tried to remember the three pages of lesson notes she had written out. Mercifully, a bit came back to her.

'Everybody get a ball,' she ordered, and there was an immediate scuffle around the large wicker baskets containing apparatus that stood in four corners of the Hall. William chose a large, plain red ball. Ben's was even bigger, marked like a chess board in black and white. Mary's was smaller than theirs but much gayer, having stripes of red, yellow and blue.

35

'Space yourselves out,' snapped Miss Grimscuttle. 'In SILENCE!'

When this had been done she said, 'Commence bouncing on the spot – go!'

The Hall was filled with heavy thuds as the children set to work. Some of the balls bounced well, but some were old and had lost their spring, so that after the first bounce they would sink to the ground in a series of feeble little hops. Miss Grimscuttle, grinding her teeth in aggravation, decided that it wasn't her fault if the equipment was no good. She stole an apprehensive glance at Mr Clodworthy in an attempt to read his thoughts.

This wasn't easy. Mr Clodworthy's favourite sport had always been boxing, which nowadays not many schools tend to do, with the result that after a few minutes Mr Clodworthy usually forgot the Physical Training lesson that he was supposed to be inspecting and lapsed into a private daydream. So that when Miss Grimscuttle thought he was looking at her in a rather strange and critical way, he was actually wondering what he could have for his dinner.

Not knowing this, Miss Grimscuttle panicked

36

a bit and thinking she had better liven things up, started to stride round the Hall shouting, 'Bounce your ball high, then jump up to catch it before it lands! Let's see if you can send your ball to the ceiling and fly up after it, so bounce and JUMP! Bounce and JUMP!' Now Ben's ball, despite being one of the largest, had an exceptionally feeble little bounce, and he was quite out of breath from trying to make it work. He would have jumped on it if he could. The wretched thing had just flopped to the floor and dribbled away from his sore hand for at least the twentieth time, when Miss Grimscuttle's penetrating 'Bounce! Bounce!' filled the Hall.

Instantly, all the little draughts that had been whispering round corners and beneath door-ways seemed to form themselves into one cold, sharp gust that whipped in and out among the children, bearing the scent of damp peat and pine needles, and at the same time, a cat's plaintive miaow echoed down, from somewhere near the ceiling. Miss Grimscuttle looked round angrily. There was that wretched cat again! If only she knew who it belonged to, she'd certainly give that person a piece of her mind!

Her savage thoughts were abruptly ended as a small ball whizzed through the air and hit her on the nose. Another, slightly larger, appeared from nowhere and caught Mr Clodworthy a resounding smack on the side of his head. He shook it, then, suddenly reminded of his happy boxing days, sat up and began to take an interest in what was happening around him.

On hearing Miss Grimscuttle's order, Ben lifted his arm high and took a desperate swipe at his apathetic ball, determined to get it at least knee-high. To his utter joy and then bewilderment, the ball touched the floor, soared up into the air straight past his nose like a rocket bound

38

for the moon, and hit the ceiling, narrowly missing one of the round white lamp-globes hanging from it.

And Ben followed. The force of his blow had lifted his feet from the ground, and seconds later he too was travelling upwards. He put out his hands to prevent himself from cannoning into the ceiling, but quickly discovered that he could stop simply by wanting to. He started to fall gently downwards, then caught sight of William a few yards away, turning a somersault in mid-air with a huge grin on his face.

'Isn't this the most terrific fun!' cried William. 'Have you seen Mary?'

39

A ball came flying towards his head and he put out a fist to shunt it away. The air was by now full of whirling, darting balls and wriggling, shrieking children. A few were scared of what was happening, but quickly realised that as soon as they thought about it they could descend to the ground and watch the fun from there.

Most of the class, however, was enjoying its newly discovered power of flight. Mary came swimming towards them, elbowing several people out of the way.

'It's the same as before!' she cried out to William and Ben. 'Did you notice? First the wind blew, then the cat miaowed. That's the signal!'

'Looks like it,' agreed William. Putting his hands together he did a graceful dive towards the ground, just skimming the floor before turning upwards to rejoin his friends.

'I say, I could soon get used to this, it's super!' he cried, hovering on an invisible chair.

'Now I know how the birds feel when they're flying,' said Mary rapturously.

'I wonder how long it will last?' said Ben. 'As soon as old Grimscuttle sees us enjoying ourselves she'll put a stop to it.'

40

They looked down. Miss Grimscuttle was by now absolutely purple with fury. She had shouted herself hoarse ordering the children to come down but they were all making such a din that none of them could hear her. She had been buffetted from head to foot by stinging balls that seemed to have a life of their own, and felt that if things didn't return to normal soon, she would go quite mad. That ridiculous Inspector didn't

help either. He just stood there, gaping, not even appearing to notice that he was being continuously bombarded by balls. Miss Grimscuttle's twitching fingers closed thankfully around her whistle, and she blew a shrill blast. At once, all activity in the air became suspended, and more than two dozen pairs of eyes turned downwards.

'Come here at once!' croaked Miss Grimscuttle, feeling uncomfortably like a worm that had suddenly been seen by a flock of starlings. In silence, like large soft snowflakes falling from the sky, children and balls slowly descended and came to rest on the floor. The lovely, light-limbed sensation vanished the moment their feet touched the ground, and regretfully, William, Ben and Mary knew that their flying had come to an end.

Shaking in every limb Miss Grimscuttle turned fearfully towards Mr Clodworthy. But she needn't have worried, because, to her amazement, he was gazing at her with an expression of undisguised admiration.

'Absolutely astonishing, my dear lady!' he exclaimed. 'I can't imagine how on earth you got them to do that, but I should like to arrange for you to come and share your secret with some other teachers at one of my meetings.'

And then he hurried off to surprise Mr Meek with the news that Miss Grimscuttle's lesson had been the best he had ever seen.

As for Miss Grimscuttle, the affair made her more bad-tempered than ever because although she couldn't think how, and certainly had no intention of asking, she was convinced that somehow or other the children had played a very clever trick upon her. So she cut the lesson short, ordered them back to the classroom and listened with inward satisfaction to their muffled groans of disappointment when she told them to take out their English Grammar text books and do exercises sixteen, seventeen, eighteen, nineteen AND twenty, before they could go out to play.

Chapter Five

GREAT GEK,
THE DRAGON

It was well on into foggy November when Mr Meek sent round a note asking all the staff to decide on an item for their class to perform in the end-of-term Christmas concert, and to start rehearsals as soon as possible. At this there was a great deal of grumbling among the teachers because they hadn't been given much time to think, but Miss Grimscuttle, who had secretly been planning for weeks, gave a smug smile.

44

Stalking in to the classroom after prayers one morning she slapped down an armful of books and demanded, 'Now listen, everybody!'

'Oh, what now?' whispered Ben to Mary, and fixing the two of them with a glare, Miss Grimscuttle snapped, 'To begin with, Ben can stay in at playtime and write out thirty times "I must not talk" and Mary can write, "I must not listen".' She had no sooner finished speaking than a sudden powerful draught forced its way through the keyhole and blew a large sheaf of papers off her table.

When they had finally been gathered up and order restored, Miss Grimscuttle went on, 'Now, the contribution that we are going to make to the Christmas Concert is the musical interpretation of a poem. You all know "Great Gek, the Dragon", but just to refresh your memory, here it is again.'

Clearing her throat she began:

'Down in a cavern
Dark and deep,
Gek the dragon
Lay asleep.

There came to his ears
A sudden noise –
The shouts and cheers
Of girls and boys.

"I'll go and see them,"
Great Gek said,
Rising up from
His stony bed.

With rattling scales
And breath of flame,
He went to join
Their happy game.

With swishing tail
And claw-tipped feet
He lumbered down
The village street.

He smiled his best
As he tried to say,
"Please be my friends
And let me stay."

But his eyes glowed red
And his teeth shone white,
And the children ran
Away in fright.

For the truth was then
As it is today –
Dragons and children
Cannot play.'

Miss Grimscuttle lowered the book and looked over the top of her glasses.

'For some time,' she said proudly, 'I have been working to set that poem to music, so that the people with the best voices can form a small choir and sing the words, while I accompany them on the piano. Some others will take the part of village children and perform a little dance, and

those who are unable to do either of those things,' she sniffed, 'will be trees in the forest.'

Ben had just decided that he would rather be a tree than anything else, when Miss Grimscuttle announced that he and William and Mary and a few more were to be in the choir, and that they would begin rehearsing on Saturday morning in the school Music Room.

'Saturday morning!' complained Mary later, as they walked home for lunch. 'My mum was going to take me into town to buy me a new dress, but now I suppose I shall have to wait till next week.'

'Ben and me were going to try and finish my boat,' said William, 'so that we could take it down to the pond on Sunday. It's a dirty trick.'

'And a fat lot of good it'll do moaning to our parents,' grumbled Ben. 'They think old Grimscuttle can do nothing wrong.'

'Never mind, perhaps we'll all catch laryngitis and lose our voices before then,' said Mary hopefully. But of course, they didn't, and on Saturday morning, dutifully assembled in the Music Room with the other chosen members of the choir.

Miss Grimscuttle was already there, rehearsing on the piano her newly-composed accompaniment to 'Great Gek, The Dragon'.

'Come along, you're late!' she exclaimed, springing up from the stool as Ben, William and Mary walked reluctantly in.

'Well, *somebody* has to be last,' thought Ben, and he longed to say it out loud, but didn't dare.

Miss Grimscuttle then set about pushing, pulling and prodding the children to the places in which she wanted them to stand. Then they sang the poem over and over, line by line, verse by verse, becoming gradually more confident until at last, Miss Grimscuttle was almost satisfied.

'That was much better,' she said, with grudging praise. 'Now we'll do the whole thing again right through, and this time I want everyone to think hard about the story, so that with our singing, we bring Great Gek the dragon to life!'

In the act of striking the first chord, Miss Grimscuttle's fingers froze upon the piano keys, for a piercing yowl rang through the air. The invisible cat once more! She wondered if it belonged to Mr Fretstone, the caretaker, and was actually living in one of the school storerooms.

Miss Grimscuttle shuddered at the thought.

The sound of the cat's voice was immediately followed by a wind which swept round the Music Room making everybody wrinkle up their noses in distaste, as it smelled of dank, unwholesome places far beneath the surface of the earth. Ben, William and Mary looked at one another knowingly, and wondered what was going to happen next.

As the wind died away and the cat (wherever it was) lapsed into silence, Miss Grimscuttle straightened her back and began to play. Dutifully, the children sang. They had just finished the fifth verse, and had taken a deep breath through wide open mouths to begin the sixth, when a faint but distinct rattle penetrated the air.

Miss Grimscuttle stopped. Angrily she whirled round and glared at Ben.

'How dare you play about during my lesson!' she yelled.

52

'Please Miss,' stammered Ben, bewildered and rather offended, 'it wasn't me.'

'Don't tell fibs!' snapped Miss Grimscuttle. 'You are the most disobedient boy in the class, so it *must* have been you. Whyever I asked you to be in the choir I can't imagine! Bring whatever you were rattling to me AT ONCE!'

'Please Miss, it wasn't Ben,' said William, hastening to his friend's defence. 'I was watching him, and he didn't move.'

'Do not answer back!' stormed Miss Grimscuttle. 'Come out to me, you naughty, disobedient boys!'

Dejectedly, Ben and William moved forward together, but hardly had they taken two steps then the rattle was repeated, this time much louder, and accompanied by a regular dull thudding. It sounded like a gigantic sledgehammer flattening the ground.

Miss Grimscuttle swung round and stared wildly at the children, her mouth open ready to shout. But they gazed back at her, wide-eyed, hands by their sides, innocently empty.

53

The rattling and thudding increased. Miss Grimscuttle leapt up from her stool and the children exclaimed aloud in confusion. The ground shook, the windows vibrated, the lamps suspended from the ceiling danced up and down.

There was a sudden loud hiss, and a blast of hot smoke mingled with orange flame shot past the window. Then, with a roar that shook the room to its very foundations, a dragon looked in.

Chapter Six

DRAGON FIRE

'Aaaaaaaaargh!' shrieked Miss Grimscuttle. 'What is it?'

The dragon blinked at the children and they inspected him with curiosity. The moment they saw his glowing red eyes and the curls of smoke idling gently skywards from his nostrils, they knew who he was.

'Don't worry, it's only Gek,' said William soothingly in the direction of the piano, behind which Miss Grimscuttle was now hiding, her usual icy composure in shreds. 'He wants to play with us.'

'D-don't be an idiot, child,' stammered Miss Grimscuttle. 'That's just a poem.'

'But you said you wanted us to make Great Gek come to life,' insisted Ben, 'and now we have.'

Miss Grimscuttle glared at Ben as though she wished the dragon would swallow him.

55

'That is impossible!' she declared, peering fearfully round the corner of the piano. 'It must be some wicked kind of trick.'

Gek caught sight of her and blew out a friendly blast of flame which scorched the window-frame and blackened the edges of the glass. Miss Grimscuttle dodged out of sight once more.

'Oh do stop it, Gek!' cried William, hurrying across the room. 'You'll set us on fire!'

Gek opened his huge mouth and grinned at William with teeth like enormous icicles.

'He only wants to play with us,' said William, 'exactly like it says in the poem.'

'Poor old thing,' said Mary sympathetically. 'I wish he could, don't you?'

'It's absolutely no use,' said Ben. 'He couldn't even get inside the door, and if he did he'd burn the place down with his breath.'

By now all the children were crowding round the window. Gek towered outside it, his great bulk rising into the air. The greenish-grey scales on his back were as hard and brittle as roof slates, and made a dry, rasping sound every time he moved. On seeing so many children he became more and more excited. Lifting up a gigantic

56

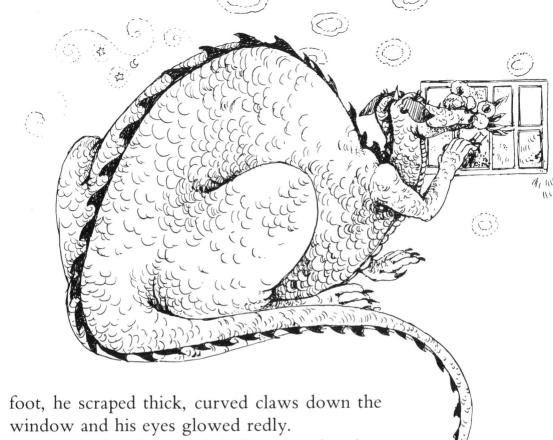

foot, he scraped thick, curved claws down the window and his eyes glowed redly.

'Stop it, Gek!' shouted William, as the glass rattled. 'You're too strong!'

'And besides, you can't stay here because certain people won't understand,' added Ben, stealing a sly, sidelong glance at Miss Grimscuttle.

The dragon listened and his ears drooped. The joyful glow faded from his eyes and he hung his head.

'It's such a shame,' said Mavis. 'We woke him up with our music, and he came all the way from his dark, stony cavern, just to play with us. I think we ought to let him have one dance, at least.'

'Oh, all right,' agreed William, who seemed to have taken charge. 'But we've got to stay in here, because he might forget and breathe fire in our direction by accident.'

He looked over at Miss Grimscuttle, who was standing up and leaning weakly against the piano in a kind of trance.

'Please, Miss Grimscuttle,' said William politely, 'would you play "Here We Go Round The Mulberry Bush"?'

Obediently Miss Grimscuttle slid on to the piano stool and with trembling fingers, played. The children joined hands and danced and sang, while outside in the yard Gek lumbered round rattling his tail and swaying his huge head in time to the music, and blowing flames into the air as high as they would go.

When the song ended William went over to the window and called, 'Gek, I'm afraid you'll have to go home now!'

At that, the dragon snorted and pawed the ground. Twin clouds of bitter black smoke poured from his nostrils. His eyes were like dark rubies.

'Oh my goodness, he's getting angry!' exclaimed Mary.

'He doesn't want to go,' said Ben. 'What shall we do?'

William thought for a moment then said decisively, 'There's only one way that I can see. We shall have to sing him back, the same as we brought him here. Miss Grimscuttle, play loudly please. Everybody, start singing from where we left off, as loudly as you can!'

Miss Grimscuttle began to pound the piano as though her very life depended upon being heard five miles away. The children sang till Ben thought his throat would burst with the effort.

'He smiled his best
As he tried to say,
"Please be my friends
And let me stay."

But his eyes glowed red
And his teeth shone white,
And the children ran
Away in fright.

For the truth was then
As it is today –
DRAGONS AND CHILDREN
CANNOT PLAY!'

The children stopped, panting from their efforts, as the final note diminished into silence. Then, hurrying apprehensively over to the window, they saw with relief the last defiant shred of the dragon's smoke fading away. Great Gek had gone.

61

'Oh,' said Miss Grimscuttle. 'Oh, oh, oh. That was terrible. Terrible!' She clutched her head.

'Please Miss, I thought we sang it rather well,' said Ben with a cheeky grin.

But Miss Grimscuttle hardly heard him. She was too busy wondering how on earth she would explain to Mr Meek the scorched window frame, the scratched and blackened glass and the cracks in the tarmac of the yard. She really needn't have worried, though, because long before Monday morning every sign of Great Gek's visit had completely disappeared.

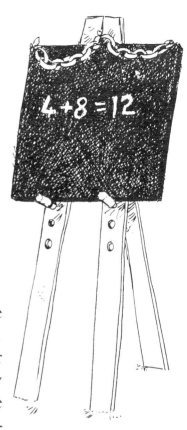

Chapter Seven

MISS GRIMSCUTTLE HAS MATHEMATICS

Two days before the Christmas holidays were due to begin, every class was in a festive mood. That is, all except Miss Grimscuttle's. The other teachers had festooned their rooms with gay decorations, balloons and bells, made by the children, but in Miss Grimscuttle's the decorations were extremely sparse.

She did not believe in wasting time on such frivolities, only allowing the children to make paper chains when they had finished the work she set them. And of course, she always set them so much that only the very quickest and cleverest had time to stick the coloured strips together, with the result that there was one single short paper chain to brighten up the whole classroom. Grudgingly, Miss Grimscuttle pinned it over the top of the blackboard.

'Please, Miss Grimscuttle,' said Mavis, raising her hand, 'all the other classes are playing games this afternoon instead of doing lessons.'

Miss Grimscuttle's mouth set into a straight line, her expression severe.

'I do not believe in games,' she declared. '*I* shall have mathematics instead.'

No sooner had she spoken than a wind so cold it seemed to have come straight across the icebergs from the North Pole, actually bringing with it tiny flurries of snow, whistled round the room, dislodging the paper chain and sending it rustling to the floor. A cat miaowed plaintively, and Miss Grimscuttle's hair stood on end with rage.

'That cat again!' she yelled. 'Everybody, search beneath your desks!'

Ben, William and Mary ducked underneath their desks and grinned at each other upside down.

64

'I wonder what's going to happen now?' whispered Mary, because as they had already guessed, the wind and the cat's voice meant that something strange was about to take place.

But rather to the children's disappointment, nothing did happen, at least, not immediately. A thorough search failed, of course, to reveal the cat, and before long the class was working hard once more. It wasn't until William went up to get his book marked that he began to understand.

As Miss Grimscuttle was frowning down at the page and covering it with a shower of little red ticks, William happened to glance at her face. Then, he stared hard, because there was a number on her forehead. It was a quite distinct number six, glowing red and angry-looking, like a measle. As he watched, a number two appeared, a little higher up, then a five sprang out on her cheek and a seven close to her ear. Before she had finished marking his page, Miss Grimscuttle's face was simply spotted with numbers. William thought rapidly back to the moment just before the wind blew and the cat miaowed. What had Miss Grimscuttle said? They had been talking about the end-of-term games and she had said, 'I won't have games, I WILL HAVE MATHEMA-TICS.'

Well, now she's jolly-well got them, thought William, and it serves her right.

Just then, for the very first time, Miss Grimscuttle noticed the fact for herself. The hand that was busily covering William's page with little red ticks (and it has to be admitted, a few crosses as well) was itself becoming covered with different sized eights and fours and sevens, and a particularly large and alarming nine. Catching sight of them, Miss Grimscuttle dropped her pen and gaped. She tried to rub off the numbers, but they wouldn't budge. She pulled up her sleeve and there they were, right up her arm. She frantically examined the other, which was even worse, as it included an isosceles triangle and a precise parallelogram. Then she dragged a small mirror from her handbag and looked at her face. Stifling a screech with difficulty she turned to William and

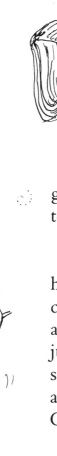

gasped, 'I'm going straight home. Please run and tell Mr Meek.'

Then she got up and rushed out of the room.

It was with great reluctance that Mr Meek left his cosy office, with its glowing electric fire, the crossword that he was on the point of solving and the cup of steaming cocoa his secretary had just made, to go and look after Miss Grimscuttle's class. He listened to William's story about the Mathematics and decided that Miss Grimscuttle must have gone mad.

Really, she was the most trying woman he had ever met. Having at first given the impression of being extremely efficient, she had turned out to be more trouble than the rest of his school put together. He, for one, wouldn't be sorry if she decided to leave. Closing his office door firmly to keep in the warm air, Mr Meek hurried through the bleak corridor to William's classroom.

Seating himself at Miss Grimscuttle's desk he said, 'Well, just get on with whatever you were doing.'

Boldly, Ben put up his hand.

'Please sir,' he said, 'all the other classes have stopped working and they're playing games.' Mr Meek blinked thoughtfully at Ben for a few seconds then said, 'Well, I don't see why you shouldn't.' Then he added, 'As long as you organise them for yourselves.' He suddenly saw a good opportunity to slip back to his office and fetch the cup of cocoa.

With William, Ben and Mary taking charge, the desks and chairs were quickly stacked around the edges of the room and the games began. They had Simon Says, with the winners taking it in turns to be He. Then they had Squeak Piggy

Squeak, the Nursery Rhyme Game, and chalking the Tail on the Donkey. Unfortunately there hadn't been time to arrange any prizes, but Mary hastily made some badges with her felt-tip pens, some paper and a few safety-pins from the needlework cupboard, saying WINNER, which seemed to satisfy everybody.

Mr Meek had just glanced at his watch and opened his mouth to say, 'Start clearing up', when Ben happened to look out of the window and see that it was snowing. He gave a loud whoop of excitement and rushed across to the window with the rest of the class behind him. They stared up at the enormous flakes falling thickly from a dark grey sky. Already the ground and trees and rooftops were covered in white.

'Perhaps, when Miss Grimscuttle sees this snow she'll decide to stay at home tomorrow,' said Mary hopefully.

'Especially,' said William, 'if she hasn't got rid of the Mathematics.'

Chapter Eight

MONKEY BUSINESS

But although everybody was hoping like mad that she wouldn't, Miss Grimscuttle turned up at school the next morning as usual. All her Mathematics had disappeared, except for a very faint scar in the shape of a number nine, still visible on the back of one hand. The afternoon off had done nothing to improve her temper, which was fanned into flame the instant she entered the classroom and her eyes lit upon the chairs and tables which Mr Fretstone the caretaker had left stacked round the room, thinking Miss Grimscuttle must have had a special reason for putting them there.

Steaming with anger she rushed to the window and banged on it, and William, Ben and Mary who happened to be passing, inwardly quaked as the bony finger of Miss Grimscuttle beckoned them to her.

72

'Gosh, she looks like a volcano about to erupt!'
breathed Ben, as they hurried down the corridor.

'And *what* is my furniture doing in *this* state?'
screeched Miss Grimscuttle, almost before they
had turned into the doorway.

Between them, the children stammered out
the story of the classroom games, and when they
had finished Miss Grimscuttle roared, 'You
naughty, disobedient children, how *dare* you
defy me! Well, I'll teach you to make a monkey
out of me!'

73

Of course, you will have guessed already what happened next. In the wink of an eye, in the very act of reaching forward with outstretched arms to make a grab at Ben, there was a miaow, a sudden breath of frozen wind, and Miss Grim-scuttle had vanished. In the very spot where she

had been standing, was a chimpanzee.

It stared up at the children and they stared down at it. Then, curling back its lips it gibbered a monkey message, jumped up and down in an excited way then leapt through the open door.

'Oh my goodness!' cried Mary. 'What shall we do?'

'Quick, we've got to follow her!' said William, and all together they dived after the chimpanzee. By the time they got outside she had disappeared.

'Gosh, I hope she doesn't head for the playground,' said Ben. 'We shall have an awful job explaining her to the others.'

But fortunately the chimpanzee hadn't gone that way, as a row of monkey footprints in the snow indicated, and following them, the children soon located her loping towards the school gates.

'She's going out into the street!' gasped Mary in horror.

'Quick, we mustn't lose sight of her!' said William, and shoulder to shoulder they sprinted up the drive. The traffic warden, just about to park his lollipop against the school railings and go home, grunted with horror as the chimpanzee scurried across in front of him, and almost dropped his STOP sign on the bonnet of a waiting car.

Ben, William and Mary hurried after her, their breath making small white clouds on the dry, frosty air, as the chimpanzee, her pace apparently unhindered by the deep snow, headed steadily away from the school and down the road. Suddenly the children saw her stop, stare, and then leap the wall into a garden where a baby sat in a pram near its front door, all bundled up against the cold, and cuddling a brown teddy-bear.

The chimpanzee eyed the baby and the baby scowled back.

'Ooo-ooo-ooo-uhh-uhh,' said the chimpanzee, which meant, 'Give me your teddy-bear.'

'Goo-ubble-ahh-hic,' replied the baby, which meant, 'I jolly well won't.'

At that, the chimpanzee sprang at the pram and seized the teddy-bear by one leg.

76

A fearful tug-of-war ensued, during which the chimpanzee screamed and bared her teeth with rage, and the baby shrieked and grew crimson in the face with anger, and in the end the teddy-bear's leg came off and the chimpanzee bowled over backwards in the snow. From somewhere inside the house a dog set up a loud barking, and Ben, suddenly remembering what an extremely large and unfriendly animal it was, went weak at the knees with fear.

As the chimpanzee, gripping the teddy-bear's leg, picked herself up and prepared to do battle with the baby for the rest of it, the front door was opened and the dog hurtled out. Its hair stood on end when it saw the chimpanzee, who, teeth bared in fury at having been cheated out of a second chance at the teddy-bear, snatched the woolly hat from the baby's head instead and leapt the wall. Then she scuttled rapidly away down the street, leaving both baby and dog almost hysterical with rage.

Ben, William and Mary hurried along behind. The chimpanzee was now going towards the shops, and upon reaching the first one which happened to be a butcher's, she hopped in at the door. By the counter stood a small, frail old lady waiting to be served with a pound of sausages. The butcher, whose speciality was home-made ones which he had at that very moment run out of, was busy in the corner making some more. When the chimpanzee jumped in through the doorway the butcher's mouth dropped open in disbelief, and he glanced down just in time to stop his fingers following the sausage-meat into the machine.

78

The small frail old lady peered short-sightedly at the creature which had appeared beside her, thinking it was a woman wearing a fur coat and a woolly hat (which in a way, of course, it was).

'Good morning, my dear,' she said, kindly. 'Although perhaps I shouldn't say "good", since the price of everything seems to have gone up again.'

'Ooo-ooo-uhh-uhh-uhh,' said the chimpanzee, eyeing the old lady's shopping basket, from the rim of which poked a mouth-watering bunch of bananas.

'My word, you do have a bad cough,' said the old lady with concern. 'Now, I know a very good —' But before she had time to recommend her favourite medicine, the chimpanzee had snatched the bananas and was whipping away down the street.

Chapter Nine

GOODBYE, MISS GRIMSCUTTLE

Ben, William and Mary came skidding round a corner just in time to see her rush out of the shop, chased by the butcher and the old lady, who was almost in tears over her stolen fruit. The old lady soon hobbled to a halt, and it wasn't long before the butcher, who was very fat and hadn't run for years, had to give up as well because he developed a stitch.

The chimpanzee dodged cunningly down an entry, but left behind a trail of discarded banana skins which were easy for the children to follow.

Emerging from the entry at the other end, they were horrified to see the chimpanzee join a queue of people shuffling slowly on to a bus which had drawn up at the stop. With their last remaining ounce of strength, Ben, William and Mary sprinted for the bus and collapsed in a heap on the platform, just as the conductor was ringing the bell.

Before anybody had time to realise what kind of animal she was, the chimpanzee scurried upstairs, closely followed by the three children. The only other occupants of the top deck were a lady and a small dog, and the moment the chimpanzee saw them she began behaving in a most disgraceful manner. Still smarting from her treatment at the baby's house she set about trying to terrorise the little dog by curling back her lip and pulling awful faces, gibbering and screeching at the top of her voice and leaping about all over the seats.

'Oh, oh, what is it?' squealed the lady, turning pale and scooping up the little dog, which yapped bravely at the menacing chimpanzee.

'Look, we've got to get her off this bus,' said William. 'Did you notice where it was going?'

'No,' answered Ben, raising his voice above the din.

'Well I did, and it said, "The Zoo",' said William.

'Oh crumbs, if she gets in among all the other monkeys we'll never find her again!' cried Mary.

'Does this creature belong to you?' exclaimed the lady, holding her handbag ready to cuff the chimpanzee if it came any nearer.

'Well, sort of, that is, we know where she ought to be,' said William. 'The trouble is, she keeps getting away from us.'

'If you could sell us your little dog's collar and lead we could take her back,' said Ben. He dug in his pockets and discovered four and a half pence, and William was just searching to see what he could add to that amount when the lady said, 'Please, don't bother to pay me, you can have them if you'll just get that animal away from here.'

She unfastened her little dog's collar with shaking fingers, and then a frantic chase ensued over the top deck as Ben and William hurried to get the chimpanzee tethered before the conductor appeared wanting to know the cause of all the bother, while Mary guarded the stairs to stop her escaping again.

At last they got her cornered, and the lady called fearfully, 'Mind it doesn't bite you!'

'She won't bite us,' said William grimly, and he snapped the collar firmly round the chimpanzee's scrawny neck. One she realised that she was a captive at last, the chimpanzee sat quietly until the bus halted at the next stop. Leading her swiftly down the stairs the children hurried back to school through the snow, casting frequent anxious glances down to see if the chimpanzee had changed back into Miss Grimscuttle yet. When they arrived at the school gates and she still hadn't, they wondered what on earth they should do.

'We can't take her in like this,' said Mary.

'Perhaps we ought to have gone to the Zoo after all,' said Ben.

'But Ben, we couldn't,' said Mary reproachfully. 'I should have awful nightmares, thinking of her locked up in a cage with real monkeys, no matter how horrid she is.'

They were still standing there wondering what to do when Mrs Boffy, having just finished her Christmas shopping, happened to walk by on the other side of the road.

She took in the situation at a glance, and noting the worried expressions on the children's faces, decided that Miss Grimscuttle's punishment had gone far enough.

Making an almost imperceptible but very complicated sign with one gloved hand, Mrs Boffy muttered a strange and extremely magic word beneath her breath.

'You've done well, Peterkin,' she said, and purring loudly a black cat, or at least its tail and two back legs, rubbed contentedly against Mrs Boffy, looking positively weird until the rest of it appeared.

So the spell was broken at last. And there stood Miss Grimscuttle staring down at them with the baby's woolly hat, now miles too small, perched precariously on top of her head, and a collar round her neck with William gripping the end of the lead.

And she knew. She KNEW.

The three children inwardly quaked. William dropped the lead as if it had suddenly burst into flames. They waited for the storm to break around their heads, but it never came. Miss Grimscuttle merely said in a rather tired voice, 'I believe that the time has finally arrived for me to retire. I shall go and live in the country on my sister's farm. Please go and tell Mr Meek that I have decided to leave immediately.'

With that she removed the collar and the woolly hat, handed them to William and strode away. And the children never saw her again.